THE MANDANA POEMS AND OTHERS

Also by Michael Wynne-Parker

Bridge Over Troubled Water

Now in its Second Edition

'Fascinating... Michael Wynne-Parker tells it all so clearly and with such authority'.

— Harpers and Queen

THE MANDANA POEMS AND OTHERS

Michael Wynne-Parker

The Book Guild Ltd
Sussex, England

This book is sold subject to the condition that it shall not, by way of trade or otherwise, be lent, re-sold, hired out, photocopied or held in any retrieval system or otherwise circulated without the publisher's prior consent in any form of binding or cover other than that in which this is published and without a similar condition including this condition being imposed on the subsequent purchaser.

The Book Guild Ltd,
25 High Street,
Lewes, Sussex

First published 1998
© Michael Wynne-Parker 1998

Set in Times
Typesetting by Raven Typesetters, Chester
Printed in Great Britain by
Bookcraft (Bath) Ltd, Avon

A catalogue record for this book is
available from the British Library

ISBN 1 85776 338 6

For Mandana

CONTENTS

Introduction		ix
Part I		1
1	I Met A Girl At Annabel's	3
2	For Mandana	5
3	Absent Princess	7
4	An Effort	9
5	When We Are Old	11
6	Early Morning Mandana	13
7	Metaphysical Mandana	15
8	Secure Within The Storm	17
9	Poem	19
10	Understanding Mandana	21
11	True Love	23
12	Princess	25
13	Request	27
14	Night Thoughts (A Dream)	29
Part II		31
15	The Alcoholic	33
16	Meditation	35
17	There Is No Death	37
18	A Glimpse Of Happiness	39
19	Round & Round The Outdoor School	41

20	A Little Sentimentality Secures Our Humanity	43
21	On Seeing Truth In A Child	45
22	A Lost Child	47
23	Norwich Cathedral	49
24	Observation	51
25	President Premadasa	53
26	Dushambe	55

INTRODUCTION

The Mandana Poems are love poems – pure and simple. The perceptive reader will, however, discover an esoteric theme running through them.

Mandana and I, though born of diverse monotheistic cultures, believe in pre-existence, seeing it as a logical precursor of belief in an afterlife. Thus we see a significance in events.

The early poems also reflect a metaphysical theme which continues in my personal tribute to President Premadasa of Sri Lanka who I knew well, admired and who was tragically blown into a million pieces by a suicide bomber.

With a Persian wife I had to include in this volume a poem written in the heartland of ancient Persia – now known as Central Asia – wherein, despite years of communism and centuries of Islam, statues of the ancient Persian poets and philosophers survive the test of time. What a discovery! The best we find in life has remained, unchanged, since earliest times.

London, July, 1996

PART I
THE MANDANA POEMS

I MET A GIRL AT ANNABEL'S

I met a girl at Annabel's
and something stirred in me.
Courage prevailed
I spoke to her
'Will you dance with me?'
Surprise indeed! – That she agreed
Agreed to dance with me.

I danced with a girl at Annabel's
as I have never danced before.
Magic was in the air that night
as we whirled across the crowded floor.
We moved as one
And time stood still
Could one have asked for more?

Yes, the girl I met at Annabel's,
who danced again with me
whose hand I held
and smile beheld
said 'Speak truth to me'.
And then I knew
a stirring true within the
depth of me.

Then I resolved
under her gaze
true to her to be.

                          5 March 1990

FOR MANDANA

I sought you down the years
and looked for you in many places
and searched for *your* eyes in varied faces.

I never knew contentment as I seemed to search in vain
for *you* – unknown but known.

Passing pleasures seemed to dull the pain
of loneliness
but could not satisfy the heart that looked
for *you*.

For how could I fulfilment find
without my friend of long ago?
And how could I know peace of mind
unless entwined
within the fabric of your love?

And never need I search again
and wander aimlessly about
For you are here
my heart's desire –
and my pleasure is to please you –
Evermore.

London, Easter 1990

ABSENT PRINCESS

Singapore without you is like
    a picture without colour
    a book without a theme
    a rose which has no scent

But it holds a happy memory
of our being here together
standing on our balcony
looking out into the future

                                      2 August 1990

Sri Lanka without you
is a crown bereft of its priceless jewel.

                                      5 August 1990

London is dead without you

                     *   *   *

Persia is a land as yet unknown
except through fleeting impressions given to me by you.

This is a canvas ready to portray the perfect picture yet to be created.

Oh Happy World when you are there!

AN EFFORT

Please forgive me dearest love
if I seem to cling to you.
And please forgive me if I am
monopolising too.

This is a fault in me I know
and out of it I would like to grow —
but, please, understand its reason.

In you I have perfection found
evoking such a love profound
unique it is
and thus I cling
to protect and hold that precious thing
and cherish it for evermore.

So help me now in love with you
as hand in hand through life we go
to recognise that freedom true
in love comes to fulfilment.

                        10 September 1990

WHEN WE ARE OLD

Old together we will be
united in tranquillity
and looking back
we shall view the road we travelled down together.

Mysteriously we met one night
since when our love has grown
– attraction, passion, friendship known
and blended all in one
fulfilment bringing.

Old together we will be
led by the hand of destiny
we conquered fears
and walked into the golden years
content to be together.

                              10 November 1990

EARLY MORNING MANDANA

No sweeter sight I have seen
than your face
when sleeping you contented lie.

A wisp of hair disturbs you.
Your eyelids quiver –
and I wonder
where are you now in your dreams?

Where ever you are
I feel the warmth of you
and your warmth fills me *with deep peace*
The peace of deep abiding love.

                Los Angeles, 7 January 1991

METAPHYSICAL MANDANA

No veil can conceal the beauty of your presence
and in the mirror of the beauty of your body I do see
Beauty Supreme – the beauty of eternity.
And in that mirror I behold myself
and am ashamed at what I see!
Hence my frustration!

For you are free as wind and pure as air
and I still tied to selfish thoughts.
Whilst you are Nature's child
I am stillborn
and wait to be alive.

Like the wind I cannot hold you
but still I am drawn along by your influence
I know not where.

And as in your body I have known your soul
I still feel the sweet presence of your beauty
lingering with me
until we meet again.

>   16 February 1991

SECURE WITHIN THE STORM

Wherever the ship
that carries my love may sail
however far away
however rough the sea
however strong the wind may blow
however high the waves
she may be calm
within the storm
and confident.

For she knows the anchor
she can rely on
is there
to hold the ship secure
until the tempest ceases
and she is safe
forever.

13 May 1991

POEM

Surpassing all women
full of sensual delights
and spiritual fulfilment
Mandana reigns supreme.

Tajikistan, The Land of
Persian Poets
13 October 1991

UNDERSTANDING MANDANA

How can I sing your praises
sufficiently to describe you
my beautiful one?

How can I describe the rare gift you bring
to life
to me?

Beyond words to describe
are your virtues
and no art can capture your spirit.

No prison bars can hold you
nor the arms of man constrain you.
None can contain you
Free and wondrous spirit
within the person
of the one I love.

                        23 December 1991

TRUE LOVE

Weak though the foundations of human love are
True Love can be built thereon
from which, in time,
The Perfect shall be.

True Love cannot be confined
Nothing can limit it.
Even fear gives way to it.
It cannot be destroyed.

True Love continually finds ways of expressing itself
and like the green shoots of Spring,
which cannot be restrained,
True Love will manifest itself.

True Love is potentially Perfect Love
and exists to convince The Beloved
that it is ultimately selfless.

Let the Beloved be joyful
when True Love is found
for put to the Test
IT WILL NOT FAIL!

> For Mandana on her birthday
> 30 March 1993

PRINCESS

I see your name
inscribed by golden pen
within the pages of the book of life.
And thus you have achieved
the accolade reserved for those
who true nobility of soul
possess
despite their natural earthiness –
and which of these attracts me most?
I do not know.
The combination of the two
the blessed God has given you;
most beauteous body
and pure soul
immersed in you I am made whole.

And now I rise
my hand in yours
to nobler ways
and higher aims.
Your love completes in me
our mutual destiny.

REQUEST

Upon my shoulder rest your head
my love
and know that I am yours
to help
and to support you.
For you I will be strong
and true
so rest your head upon my shoulder now
and smile your lovely smile
and sing a Persian song for me.

NIGHT THOUGHTS (A Dream)

In my arms at night you lie
peaceful calm serene
and I wonder
when I die
who will hold you then?

A child we know
a child we love
he shall hold your hand
and he will whisper in your ear
words you understand

And he unites us through the years
and smiles at you
and calms your fears

Out of our dreams
that charm the night
memories mingle
thoughts unite
and LOVE is born again.

PART II

THE ALCOHOLIC

An unhappy story
  of vainglory
    and of fear.

  Fear of the night
 the endless night
of solitude.

  Men see the show
 and fail to know
the inside story.

 Unhappiness
  the Human Curse
and what is worse than that?

But it opens doors
  doors of perception
    or is it deception?

  And it makes me sad
 that they think me mad.
That's all.

              Norwich 1971

MEDITATION

The air is still and calmness fills the scene.
The sun is shining on the lake.
Seagulls hover over its water still:
Moorhens echo their haunting cry.

And now a gentle breeze
and little wavelets flit across the lake.
All is still. A radiance abounds;
God is here.

The trees, no longer green, are golden now.
The sun shines on them – giving them brilliance all their own.
Autumnal richness everywhere is seen.
God is here – I am glad I've been.

Blickling, Norfolk 1972

THERE IS NO DEATH

There is no death!
Think O man
the life that is in thee is life eternal!

Observe!
The life of nature does not die ...
behold the acorn fall into the ground
decaying morbid matter.
Behold again the noble Oak arise ...
from decay emerges life – not death!

And if nature does not die
why should men be different?

There is no death!
Think O man
the life that is in thee is life eternal!

Ponder on this.
Within the outer layer of human form
the very essence of our being lies
undaunted by the prospect of the grave
it seeks to find fulfilment
here – and then in other spheres
wherein it knows no limit and no fear.

Ponder this O man
and learn
The simpler our life
the more serene our soul
the less on props we lean
the easier to receive with confidence our heritage —
to enter into life eternal
and to live!

1972

A GLIMPSE OF HAPPINESS

I have seen a glimpse of happiness.
Just a tiny glimpse on a summer evening.

It happened like this:

We went for the walk
to the top of the hill
where the earth embraces the sky.

There we felt the soft glow
of the evening sun
and listened to the sound of the gentle breeze
playing music with the leaves and the grass.

Then I felt something warm and gentle in the silence
    of the evening –
your hand in mine!

Some people seem to be happy all the time
I wonder why – I wonder how?

Possibly such people are so familiar with happiness
as to take it for granted (imagine that!).

Having not known persistent torment
they never know the moment of bliss.

Oh happiness whose presence I have fleetingly beheld
help me to know you more.

With Elizabeth
Iona 1973

ROUND & ROUND THE OUTDOOR SCHOOL

Round and round the outdoor school you rode
the wind was in your hair
the thrill and joy of your very first canter
completely removed all fear.
Tall you sat
secure and proud ...
Little did you know
that centuries ago
the thunder of your horses galloped large and free
across these lands
your natural heritage.

No wonder your pony held his head high
and felt your pride
when last you rode round the outdoor school!

1974

A LITTLE SENTIMENTALITY SECURES OUR HUMANITY

You looked at him
he understood
you mounted him
and rode him proudly
and the thrill you experienced
he felt too.
Rider and mount were one.

And when it was over
you didn't forget
his passion for apples ...

The fresh taste of that apple he now dreams of
and looks for you.

1974

ON SEEING TRUTH IN A CHILD

You speak the truth to me my little one
I see it in your eyes
It is so naturally expressed
I cannot take offence.
Your questions penetrate reality
And I am bound to answer honestly
I do not know ...

* * *

Absolute honesty is the basis of trust.
With this knowledge a child is born.

1974

A LOST CHILD

I have no tears left to weep for you
the injury that fate has wrought
has wrung from me a lifetime's tears.
Evil has conquered now,
(I know not why)
and hell has known its little day.

But hope I have
and hope there lies
a basic bond between us –
the seeds of friendship's tie,
securely rooted, none can pluck away,
Grow they will
until they provide
reunion's certainty.

Faith must conquer!

1974

NORWICH CATHEDRAL

It isn't the form of service
or the type of theology
or that it's 'high' or 'low' or 'broad'.

No it's none of those things that draw me to you
and entice me to linger within your walls

IT'S THE MUSIC

Theology is just ideas – the passing ideas of men
that speaks to the mind
– or puzzle it –
– but they rarely speak to the heart.

And the heart, not the mind, is the centre of man.

The sun shines through the windows
illuminating the noble architecture of the
ages. And revealing the well worn
pavement below.

Many have come and gone
Catholic and Protestant
'High' and 'Low'
many sermons
WORDS WORDS WORDS –
and so little remembered.
(Ever asked anyone to explain a sermon?)

The Music speaks louder than words
– and lives on for ever
It transcends the narrow
circumference of the mind
and manifests heaven.

                                    1975

OBSERVATION
(In a bar, on a ferry, on the way to France)

Into space she stares.
What is she thinking?
Not of him who sits beside her.
Her thoughts are far away
he knows not where
nor does he care.

1989

PRESIDENT PREMADASA

The Lion of his race has returned
to set his people free
Chosen son of destiny,
blest of the Triple Gem, he steps upon the
stage of history.

Nothing can deter him
wisdom will bestir him
all shall stand to hear him
as he rises to proclaim
the words that men have waited for
through years of pain ...

'Look to yourselves, you people,
and rise above your fears.
Let no foreign foe divide you
but learn from many years
that UNITY IS STRENGTH!
Arise you people of the Lion race
and grasp the hand of destiny.
No backward glance can satisfy
but, forward go with me.'

The Lion of his race has returned.
Nothing can impede his course.

Politics may divide
and petty greedy men contrive
to undermine his power.

This they shall fail to do
for the Gods have favoured you
Thrice Blest of ages gone.

With inner strength you will prevail
and the scribe of history will write
a tale
of heroism.

From every village will arise
a call for recognition
that the lion has returned,
that the humble will prevail,
that the gifts that God has given men
will be made known.
Though faithful to their native tongue
a common language shall unite
the people of this land,
and thus united
they shall put behind all fear,
all prejudice,
all ethnic tension:
Yes they shall be one.
Thus will Lord Buddha bless their land
who once upon it stepped.

Fit to proclaim message of his peace
they shall become.
Embracing all
Muslim, Christian, Hindu, Buddhist,
none shall be denied their place
in Paradise
on Earth.

Colombo, 5 August 1990

DUSHAMBE

Snow-capped hills surround the city of Dushambe
wherein there stands
a statue of Rudaki
whose gaze confronts
the crossroads of the ancient world.

Serene he remains
despite the confusion of the present time
when ideologies are torn asunder
hypocrisies revealed
and Lenin's eyes no longer view the scene.

Ancient truth remains unchanged
surviving all man's pomp and arrogance.
The influence of the ancient poets survive
a tribute to the father of them all.

Farewell Lenin
your days are done.
The more we know of you
the less we honour you

Your philosophy inspired great hopes
aroused ideas
promised a new world order
and failed.

It is the ancient Persian poets
who inspire us still.
Firdousi, Saadi, Hafez
and old Khayam
still hold their sway within the modern world.

                                            1991